# DEVOTION

# DEVOTION

## 21 DAYS OF CULTIVATING THE WINNING HABITS OF THE GOLDEN STATE WARRIORS

JONAS N. STRICKLAND

publish
your gift

Special discounts are available on bulk quantity purchases
by book clubs, associations and special interest groups.
For details email: sales@publishyourgift.com
or call (888) 949-6228.
For information log on to www.PublishYourGift.com

# TABLE OF CONTENTS

# ACKNOWLEDGMENTS

I truly am grateful and humbled for the grace extended to me by God to develop this book for the well-being of others. I would like to thank my wife, April Strickland, for the love, support, and patience that she extended in helping me complete this project as she guided our family, even while dealing with her own health challenges. I would also like to thank the brothers of the KING D.C. Chapter: President Omar Douglas for holding me accountable to complete this work; Bishop Dr. Frank Clinton for connecting me with the team at Publish Your Gift; Brother David Jackson, Sr., and Brother Eric Walker for your gracious, financial contributions to this project; and Brother Alfonso Sawyer for your encouragement and wisdom during the process. I would also like to thank my friends Krys Williams, Garrick Younger, and Reann Gordon for their thoughtfulness and feedback during my times of uncertainty and frustration.

I would like to thank the D.C. Commission of Arts and Humanities for awarding me a grant that supported the publication of this manuscript. I was truly humbled and honored to be an award recipient. Thank you for all that you do to support artists and creatives in Washington, D.C. I would like to thank my HBCU Creative Podcast family, James Davis and Cedric Johnson, for pushing me to publish my ideas. We are brothers, and I appreciate you. I would like to thank my best friend, Edmond Limes, for seeing the vision and believing in my gift. I pray God gives you the desires of your heart.

Finally, I would like to thank the team at Publish Your Gift. I connected instantly with your message, and I truly believe that no other publishing company is equipped to carry the mantle of this project to reach the world. I honor you, and the best is yet to come.

# INTRODUCTION

I fell in love with sports and sports journalism as a child growing up in Boston and Washington, DC. I really didn't enjoy reading, but my parents knew that I loved sports. To encourage my love of reading, my parents ordered my first subscription of *Sports Illustrated* when I was six. This was a pivotal moment in my life. I was drawn to the stories and images of my favorite athletes, Ervin "Magic" Johnson, Kareem Abdul-Jabbar, James Worthy, Kurt Rambis, Mychel Thompson, Michael Cooper, and Byron Scott. Yes, I was a rabid Lakers fan living in Boston, and I thought the Lakers were the greatest team in sports, with Coach Pat Riley patrolling the sidelines in the sharpest dress suits (à la the former Villanova Wildcats Coach Jay Wright).

I remember vividly my father taking me to a shoe store to purchase the "Weapon" Lakers Converse at a store in the heart of downtown Boston. The salesperson refused to sell me the shoes because I chose the purple and gold of the Lakers over the Celtics' green and white. My father was in disbelief and told the sales rep that "I was only a kid." We left the store and my father ended up purchasing me some other shoes from Payless (as I write this, I think maybe my father was glad to have walked out of the first shoe store, blaming the sales associate and their poor customer service as the reason why I couldn't wear those Laker-inspired shoes in favor of a less expensive brand). Boston has some of the world's most devoted fan bases, and as a lover of sports, I appreciate their passion because it is embedded in their daily culture, touching every facet of life in Boston and going beyond the state of Massachusetts.

My family later moved back to my parents' hometown, Washington, DC, where football became king for me as a youth in the third grade. My mother, grandparents, aunts, and uncles were loyal Washington football fans, and to antagonize them I rooted for Tony Dorsett and the Dallas Cowboys. The teams I pulled for when I was younger were the teams on television, but I later also took an interest in teams that weren't highly visible to the greater viewing audience.

Living in Washington, I watched a lot of Big East college basketball with coach John Thompson and the Georgetown Hoyas, who had a lot of great players, including Patrick Ewing, Dikembe Mutumbo, Alonzo Mourning, Charles Smith, Allen Iverson, and Victor Page, to name a few. One of the Hoyas' biggest rivals was the St. John's Redmen (later changed to the Red Storm) out of New York City, and I became a huge fan of one of their guards, Chris Mullin. Chris was a great shooter who brought competitive fire to every game. I also enjoyed watching the skillful guard play of Tim Hardaway as he orchestrated his Texas-two step crossover at the University of Texas at El Paso with coach Don Haskins. When Tim and Chris became teammates for the NBA's Golden State Warriors, I stuck my flag with the Warriors, and they became my favorite NBA team. I was a devoted Warriors fan and left the glitz and glamor of the Showtime Lakers.

Over the years, I have followed the Warriors more intently, from their classic "We Believe Team" that knocked out the number-one seed Dallas Mavericks in the first round of the 2007 NBA playoffs, to the Splash Brothers' Death Lineup and the Hamptons Five with Kevin Durant. The wins and losses taught me life lessons that I plan to share with you in this 21-day devotional.

This devotional will provide you with anecdotes from various sports writers covering the Warriors and the NBA that you can apply to your daily life. These daily devotions, which include keys to having successful relationships, directions to achieving your goals, and insights to help you fulfill your dreams, will help you to be successful in your personal life. The championship DNA of the Golden State Warriors and their strategy for victory can be imprinted on your character to achieve monumental success. Studies have shown that people can change behavior by being intentional about their actions in just 21–30 days. Sports is life, and within these pages is a blueprint that you can apply to fulfill your purpose and destiny.

Every victory and loss provides a lesson that can guide your decisions in life. There are people who make great decisions, good decisions, and bad decisions, and then there are those who are indecisive and don't decide at all—which is ultimately their decision. The more we make great and good decisions, the more we will experience daily wins and victories over challenging obstacles. This book is for athletes, Warriors fans, basketball enthusiasts, sports fans, aspiring leaders, and those who want to win in life. This is your winning season, and winning is sacred.

# DAY 1:
# ENERGY

*"He [Draymond Green] was our best player tonight. He was the guy who was bringing the energy and the life. We didn't have much energy from most of our group tonight. When you are lacking conditioning, like we are right now, you have to have high-energy guys out there. As soon as he went out of the game, things went south for us. We just couldn't get any traction."—Steve Kerr on Draymond Green and the Warriors' 122-121 loss to the Rockets (0-1), October 17, 2017*

Energy is the cornerstone and key requirement for building a lasting relationship or completing a lasting endeavor. Energy is defined as the strength and vitality required for a sustained physical or mental activity. Without energy, things can become pretty dull and routine. Energy is not based on age or gender, or even a health condition. You can be a person with limited mobility, but your mind and spirit can be fully engaged with creative energy that can change lives and impact nations around the globe. However, the greatest places that need to feel the entire force of our energy are our relationships. There have been many days when I have come home to my family and it has been challenging to engage with them due to being physically tired or mentally drained due to stress and anxiety.

We were created to be fruitful, to multiply, to increase and dominate in every area of our lives. To carry out this mandate, we require energy. The great news is that when you were created, you were equipped to fulfill this mission. Being fruitful cannot be done alone; it requires a team. When there is friction between team members or in our relationships, it can drain our enthusiasm and vitality, which has a direct impact on our energy. If the issue is not resolved, our relationships can go through a dry season that can create distance and resentment between our loved ones and team members.

The issue is not designed to bring us apart but rather is a unique gift that shines a light on an area of concern that is hindering our productivity. In the Warriors' case, it was a lack of conditioning that caused them to lose against the Rockets. Take serious inventory of the underlying causes of the issues in your relationships, and as a team, address them. Any issue that is not fruitful, cut it off and remove it so that you can be more fruitful. Going through an unproductive season will drain your energy, and your energy is needed to obtain your victory. Winning is sacred.

**Action Point**: Identify the root causes of the habits, influences, and thoughts that are not fruitful and depleting your energy.

**Declaration**: I have the energy to be like a tree that bears good fruit in every area of my life.

# DAY 2: MENTORSHIP

The Spurs concocted the most efficient offense in the league, spreading the floor with three-peat shooters, exploiting mismatches, creating off-the-ball movement, and picking defenses apart with the extra pass.

The Warriors use those same principles, only with a twist. San Antonio weaponized smart role players to compensate for an aging nucleus. Steve Kerr uses Hall of Famers at the peak of their powers. The result: two titles in three years, with a record 73-win sandwiched in between. Expect nothing less in 2017–2018: 91.4% of Golden State's offense from last year is returning (Nadkarni and Sharp 2017).

The time is now to utilize your gifts to their greatest potential. Your family, social network, the financial marketplace, and the world must experience your gifts at their peak power. Unfortunately, so many gifts are not nurtured into maturity and do not have the maximum impact on their predestined recipients. All too often, gifts wallow into inadequacy due to the lack of readily available trained teachers, coaches, mentors, insightful visionaries, and—most importantly—loving parents who can identify unique skills within us and shape them into masterpieces. These thought leaders look deep into our souls and inspire us to do more with less.

The value of mentoring and coaching is a powerful antidote that stirs up dormant goals and dreams. Past disappointments, failures, hurts, and mistakes can plant feelings of inadequacy that can minimize our talents and skills. We are to learn the principles of our past but never dwell on the memories. Memories can become a strong barrier to our present and future if a past thought defines our present identity. The significance of a mentor or coach is that they can help turn your past into a tool that can revolutionize your present. A clear head and heart can produce extraordinary results.

The faster we let go of the past and walk in our gifting, the sooner we will reach our potential. A unique gift needs to be used in its prime and not by role players. The time is now!

**Action Point**: Connect and listen intently, physically or virtually, to a mentor or life coach who can help you reach your full potential.

**Declaration**: I am free from my past and will utilize my unique and special gift(s) to impact the world for good.

# DAY 3:
# CONNECTION

*"News on Wednesday that forward Kevin Durant was out with a left thigh contusion came with a silver lining for the Warriors: For the first time this season, head coach Steve Kerr wouldn't need to deliberate over whom to make inactive. That the inactive list—a place typically reserved for injured players, players well past their prime or long-term projects—has been a source of anxiety speaks to Golden State's unrivaled depth. In the Warriors' 125-101 rout of Minnesota on Wednesday night at Oracle Arena, they showed that even the absence of an eight-time NBA All-Star is no biggie when everyone on the bench can contribute."—* Connor Letourneau, SF Gate, on the Warriors' victory over the Timberwolves, 125-101; (9-3), November 9, 2017

After winning the NBA Championship in 2017, the Golden State Warriors were considered the heavy favorites to win the Larry O'Brien trophy as back-to-back NBA champions in Kevin Durant's second season with the team. The Warriors were stacked with all-star players and savvy veterans who served as role players coming off the bench. In some instances, the players coming off the bench could have been starters for other NBA teams. The bench players sacrificed their individual playing styles for the greater good of the entire unit. This wealth of talent became a source of anxiety for Coach Steve Kerr because there were some nights when key players wouldn't be able to get any playing time. What would compel a world-class athlete in basketball or any highly qualified professional in their field to lay aside the opportunity to showcase their gifts and talents for the greater good of the team or organization? What thought or desire would urge a wife or a husband to take the second position just so their spouse could be loved or respected?

Before a leader can ever make a request from their team, they must first establish a connection with them. Within the mind of every successful leader are a vision and a strategy to fulfill that vision. The goals that are shared within a family or organization are created to bring the vision to fruition. Along the way, there will be obstacles and barriers that stifle the end goal. Connection is vital throughout the entire fulfillment of a vision but even more so during challenging times of uncertainty, because these are the times when others may question the strategy and cause division, which may require correction and discipline to be enacted for the well-being of the team. Connection steps in at this specific moment of despair and provides the necessary boldness to address any underlying issues. Connection always proceeds correction.

If the Warriors' role players weren't connected to Kerr's vision of serving as integral pieces coming off the bench, they could have caused issues that fractured the team's chemistry. Instead, they accepted their assignments and were prepared when they were called upon to play at the highest level. When families, businesses, and organizations are tightly connected by a shared vision, they are bound by an unbreakable link that is a source of strength during times of adversity. Stay connected. We are stronger together.

**Action Point**: Sacrifice is more important than status. Who do you need to serve?

**Declaration**: I have the wisdom and compassion for people to be able to genuinely connect with those in my care.

# DAY 4:
# THE STRATEGY

*"Someone had to step up, and on Monday night it was old hand Andre Iguodala, former NBA Finals MVP, and permanent curmudgeon [old man]. When the Warriors are off their collective game, his presence has often been palliative [relieving pain or alleviating a problem], a quick fix to issues that should unravel an evening."—Ethan Sherwood Strauss, ESPN, on the Warriors' victory over the Atlanta Hawks 105-100 (16-2), November 29, 2016*

Iguodala's maturity, acute knowledge of the game, and humility gave him the authority to quickly resolve issues on the court, even during times when it seemed like the Warriors were going to fall apart. His calming presence was especially needed during stretches when his teammates weren't flowing on offense or connected on defense. Iguodala mastered

26

the art of responding instead of simply *reacting* to circumstances. Responding requires us to think about the outcome of our actions and is rooted in how others will be impacted by our decisions. Reacting gives no thought to how others will be impacted; it is driven by what we feel is best regardless of the outcome. Serving as a peacemaker to resolve conflicts effectively in our lives is a learned skill. The training ground for building lasting conflict resolution is within the home. If conflict resolution is not planted appropriately within a home, rage and rash conduct will be the fruit that seeps into communities. Regardless of our family upbringings and childhood experiences, it is never too late to become a lighthouse and a calming presence in the face of adversity.

Conflict is rooted in a lack of communication. Instead of reacting to an offense with anger, impulsivity, etc., respond with power, love, and a sound mind, using the **GSW** strategy:

- **Gameplan the Situation:** Identify where the problem occurred (do not say *always*, *never*, etc.). Example: "Last night when I called you twice . . ."

- **State the Behavior:** Identify the specific behavior you saw or heard, what they physically did (do not try to determine their motive or prove what is in someone else's heart). Example: "You did not answer or return my multiple phone calls."

- **Word out the Impact:** Allow others to see how their actions made you feel. Example: "I felt disrespected."

Being an effective communicator will give you the ability to articulate your feelings with boldness while modeling for others how to deal with unresolved conflict. Whether your feelings are heard or dismissed, the importance is that you effectively communicate your thoughts on the issue. Responding rather than reacting will make you a valuable member of your team, a light in the darkness that provides leadership and calm to your family and team. Winning is sacred.

**Action Point**: Develop your personal code that shapes your heart and guides your mouth to speak life to others.

**Declaration**: My presence calms a storm and brings direction to others, even in silence.

# DAY 5:
# PRESENCE

*"Kerr's message was true enough, though. Curry, who has been top 2 in total plus-minus through four consecutive seasons, brings an impact beyond his shooting efficiency on a given night. Even cold Curry can pace the Warriors, but Golden State will herald the return of this incandescent incarnation with celebration and relief."—Ethan Sherwood Strauss, ESPN, on the Warriors' 112-105 victory over the Knicks, March 5, 2017*

The total plus-minus statistic measures the impact that a player has on his or her team when they are on the court based on their contributions on offense and defense. Coaches create starting lineups and bench rotations based on the analytics of a given player's output. More importantly, when the game is on the line, championship contenders will put the best five positional players on the court that have a plus-minus ratio that will garner their victory. Being a complete player or member of an organization who can add value to any situation speaks to the gift of presence. Your mere presence is what makes the difference in turning defeat into victory. It is more than an aura; it is a sense of calm and assurance that because you are there the experience of everyone in your vicinity has just been heightened to another level. A presence that brings life, vitality, and growth to families, friendships, and businesses is irreplaceable. More than ever, communities and neighborhoods need people who carry a presence.

For some, the presence you carry is calling you to restore your position as a leader; in other settings, all you will need to do is show up and serve with humility. In other settings, you are to take the position of a student and be teachable, and in another context, teach with accuracy. In whatever capacity or role that you encounter, cultivate and embrace your presence for the well-being of others. Quiet confidence shaped and developed in obscurity can create a lasting impression that resonates from our presence.

**Action Point:** Identify five characteristics that you want others to feel or recognize about you when you walk into a room. Begin to develop those areas in your life.

**Declaration:** I enhance the lives of everyone in my presence for good.

# DAY 6:
# THE EDGE

*"As the Warriors strove for further excellence on a team supposedly with few weaknesses, coach Steve Kerr repeated endlessly about his players' need to play with an edge. The Warriors lacked the edge to exhibit any defensive discipline. Instead, the Warriors played on edge as they became upset with the officiating, their turnovers, and the Pelicans prolific offense."—Mark Medina, The Mercury News, on the Warriors' 128-110 victory over the Pelicans (1-1), October 21, 2017*

There is a distinct difference between playing on the edge and playing with an edge. Playing on the edge is self-driven and can be hampered by our ego, pride, insecurities, fears, and our feelings about others. Playing with an edge is predicated on placing all of our energy toward completing a goal and fulfilling a purpose directed by a strategic vision. Playing with an edge looks beyond our human frailties and places a premium on every decision and action, leading to the fulfillment of the desired outcome. No matter what our shortcomings are, playing with an edge sharpens our vision away from ourselves and places us in a flow to achieve greatness. It's not about you when you play with an edge; it's about the result.

Playing with an edge represents being prepared and confident in our abilities to put our hands to the plow in order to receive a harvest, regardless of our fears, uncertainties, or the conditions of the land and surrounding environment. Playing on the edge lacks preparation and goes off-script, creating tension and edginess. It is a clear sign of mental, emotional, and spiritual blindness. Not having a sense of direction and vision is detrimental to any team, family, or organization. It often leads to tension and distrust, and with no vision, the people perish.

A crystal-clear focus that is shaped by a vision birthed in humility, that is not contaminated with ego and pride, can produce a resounding victory. Winning is sacred.

**Action Point:** Take time to self-reflect and identify any areas of your life that lack vision.

**Declaration:** I can see clearly now to live my life with an edge on purpose.

# DAY 7: GROWTH

Growth is essential to our development. We grow and mature into different levels. For example, there is a level where deciding to make a purchase (a car, vacation package, etc.) is based on the cost. There is another level where the decision is based on the value. There is another level where cost and value are insignificant, and the purchase decision is based solely on experience. A person should not look down on themselves or compare themselves to others if they are currently at a particular station in life. It is wise to be a good steward of our resources. The problem arises when we try to obtain things at a certain level we have not grown into. This is when fouls occur and we start a slow decline until we eventually lose the game. Fouls take place when we are quick to go instead of being in a flow to grow.

We foul others in our relationships by constantly arguing, having petty disagreements, making intentional slights, and being easily offended. Relationships are the keys to our success, and when our relationships are hampered due to a lack of growth, be prepared to lose the defensive stronghold that would put us in a position to score and eventually win in our families and communities. Never stop growing mentally, emotionally, spiritually, physically, and financially. Be committed to being a lifelong learner. Your growth is the determining factor that will produce a lasting victory that will silence your adversaries. Your growth worries the people who depend on your immaturity to make them look mature.

**Action Point:** Identify one area of your life that has caused you concern through self-reflection. Without condemning yourself, create a plan that will help you grow mentally in that area, leading to a transformation of the situation.

**Declaration:** I am committed to growing in every area of my life. The more I know, the more I grow.

# DAY 8:
# THE THREAT

*"Kerr's offense is much more about all five players being a threat instead of just riding the talents of one player. So often, Curry's gravity is used to force the defense to adjust and create openings for his teammates. Curry spends a lot of time running off screens away from the ball and setting back screens, using the attention he draws to grease the Warriors' offensive machine."*—Marcus Thompson, The Athletic, on the Warriors' 124-116 victory over the 76ers (12-4), November 19, 2017

There is a stark difference between making a threat and being a threat. When an individual makes a threat, they're trying to manipulate a certain outcome using their words. In some instances, the threat may be a pure bluff masked by deception. However, when an individual truly is a threat, no words need to be spoken. Their mere presence puts everyone on notice, a testament to their consistent past performances, position, and expertise honed over time. Using words to intimidate others achieves temporary results, whereas being a threat creates a legacy that endures.

Carriers of this mantle do not abuse their position to be a menace to others or society, but rather use their skills to allow members in their families, communities, and organizations to flourish in their assigned giftings. These individuals are a source of energy that draws the attention of the opposition away from their loved ones and colleagues, creating a lane for others to achieve success, confidence, and a series of victories.

A person who is considered a threat does not make boastful claims but operates in humility to serve the good of others. They are not rooted in ego or pride but are shaped in persistence and diligence to develop personal excellence and greatness. While others are drawn to the finished product, the process is what creates the grit and resilience that harden the individual to produce their outstanding results. The threat does the work and lets others speak. They have come to learn that consistent actions are resounding and make a lasting impact that produces confidence in others, even in their absence.

**Action Point**: Identify and create a plan to overcome every distraction that may be hindering your consistency in an area of needed growth.

**Declaration**: I am committed to the daily process that makes my presence comforting, yet hard as flint. I will not be ashamed.

# DAY 9:
# COMMUNICATION

Relationships are the key to our success. They provide us with opportunities to grow and examine our thoughts and motives. We achieve greatness and excel to new heights as we develop ourselves and show honor in building quality relationships. Some relationships are lasting, while others are temporary and are only for a season. The deeper the impact we seek in our relationships, the more intentional we must be in our communication. When companies have developed a system that yields outstanding results, there is a chance that complacency and routine will set in, which can cause a disruption in production and/or a lack of growth. In relationships, this can look like communication that is only centered on facts and cliches, such as "It's sure hot outside." "How was your day?" "My day was fine."

Communication that is shaped by the mundane day-to-day activities of life and does not embrace the risk of walking to the edge and being vulnerable opens the door for us to walk in denial without sharing our true feelings and needs. Denial defense is what stifled the Warriors from executing their offense, and the denial of our feelings blocks the flow of communication that is necessary for building emotionally secure relationships. This is easier said than done, as past experiences shape how people receive and share their feelings.

Being intentional about how we share our innermost thoughts requires patience, tact, and a well-thought strategy, as in a team's playbook. Before a play is executed in a game against an opponent, it is first shared in practice. Before having challenging conversations, seek the advice of someone you trust who will listen to you and provide sound counsel. Sharing your feelings with someone you trust can give you the strength to overcome rejection. The fear of rejection and the unknown of how someone will respond to our feelings are barriers that can hinder intimate communication. Practicing our delivery can provide the confidence we need to push past rejection so that we can recover and have vibrant, fresh, and fulfilling relationships.

**Action Point:** Identify an area of concern that may be blocking the flow of communication in your relationships. Seek one or two accountability partners who can provide insights into your feelings and needs.

**Declaration:** My voice is equipped to share my innermost thoughts and feelings with clarity and conviction.

# DAY 10:
# CENTER STAGE

*"Thompson hadn't been great to that point, but none of that matters in winning time. The league's stars can erase off-nights with late heroics or watch a night full of big plays crumble with a couple of backbreaking bricks. Steve Kerr called timeout with 62 seconds left. The game was tied. The plays were scripted for Thompson. He was tasked with bringing the Warriors home. Thompson failed, missing all three of his late shots, as the Warriors went scoreless in the final 3:11 and watched the 6-14 Kings pop a 10-0 run on them and escape from Oracle with a win."—Anthony Slater, The Athletic, on the Warriors' 110-106 loss to the Kings, November 27, 2017*

Challenging situations can be overcome based on our perspectives. Having the right mindset and framework as a solid foundation can serve as an advantage when we face dilemmas. Therefore, it is essential that we constantly feed our intellect with ideas, conversations, and information that nurture our "thought life" before a problem appears on the horizon. When we encounter an unexpected issue, this is life's way of opening the stage curtain to showcase our strengths to the world. Whether we are prepared or not, the show must go on.

The Golden State Warriors were without Stephen Curry and Kevin Durant, and Klay Thompson was called upon to close out the Sacramento Kings. Plays were designed to get the ball into Thompson's hand with the hope that he would be able to lead the Warriors to victory. Regardless of the outcome, the fact remains that a sequence of plays was drawn out specifically for him because of his skill level, expertise, and competence in previous contests. The situation that you are currently facing or will face has been created specifically for you to showcase your unique skills and talents. A strategy has been developed in the book of life that you must execute to secure victory. This is not the time to wallow in self-pity and ask, "Why me," but rather, the time to embrace this as your season of manifestation, to demonstrate to the world your one-of-a-kind strength that only you can perform on the stage of life.

Therefore, it is imperative that we read our script, know our lines, and engage with the producer, as well as the other cast members who play a role in the various scenes of our life. If we are not prepared or connected, it will be shown on the stage. The audience is waiting with anticipation. Give them a performance that will leave them with a lasting impression. Winning is sacred.

**Action Point:** Identify and develop at least three strengths in your life that make you unique. Use them as anchors to sustain you when you face various challenges.

**Declaration:** I manifest the greatness that produces winning results, ending all discussions.

# DAY 11:
# DECISIVENESS

*"Remember when it was the Death Lineup? The Warriors would put in their best five players and eviscerate teams. That lineup was a kill shot. And then it swapped out Harrison Barnes for Durant. So far this season, the vaunted five-man unit of Curry, Klay Thompson, Andre Iguodala, Durant, and Green has been ineffective. That unit closed the first half and the Lakers—it-would-be-a shock-if-they-make-the playoffs Lakers—went on a run. The Hamptons 5 has been emblematic of a glaring issue with the Warriors, one that Kerr has pointed out. The Warriors don't have a killer instinct right now. They aren't seeking to destroy."—Marcus Thompson, The Athletic, on the Warriors' 127-123 overtime victory over the Lakers, November 30, 2017*

After winning their second NBA title in three years and the first with Kevin Durant in the starting lineup, the Golden State Warriors were once again considered the title favorite to win the championship at the start of the 2017–2018 NBA season. Past championship-winning teams have discussed at length the physical, mental, and emotional drain that accompanies winning an NBA title and the strain that teams endure at the start of the following season to regain their championship form. This appeared to be the case with the Warriors as they began the defense of their title. Coach Kerr felt that his team did not play with a killer instinct, which allowed less talented teams to hang around in games that should not have been as competitive.

This mindset is not only common among athletes. Married couples can lose the drive to keep the fire alive in their relationship. When we have achieved success in any area of our life for an extended period, complacency can creep in and cause us to let our guard down. The key to maintaining a killer instinct—a mindset that is singularly focused on achieving a set goal on a consistent basis—all begins with a decision. A small yet significant choice that can make the difference in our daily lives is to decide to die daily to our ego, pride, and insecurities.

The Latin meaning of "-cide" is "killer" or "act of killing" (e.g., pesticide, homicide, etc.). To de*cide* to do something, we must kill a thought or an idea that does not align with our purpose. When we are indecisive or choose not to decide, we are rooted in uncertainty. Uncertainty can then lead to hesitation, and once we begin to hesitate, it slowly chips away at our edge. In fact, no matter how great our success is, it is necessary that we evaluate the motives that drive our decisions in order to experience a high level of achievement over an extended period of time. When we have a steady perspective and do not think more of ourselves or less of others, we are able to give the same level of excellence in every circumstance, regardless of our competitor, our time in a position, or the task at hand. Winning is sacred.

**Action Point:** Let your yes be *yes* and your no, *no*. Take the time to think and be decisive.

**Declaration:** I am equipped with the necessary resources to make sound decisions—decisions that keep the fire alive!

# DAY 12:
# COMPOSURE

*"Yeah, it's absolutely too much. We're not composed out there. We're a championship team. We have to execute out there. We're getting way too emotional, myself included. I've got to do a better job of that too. But we've got to show some poise when things aren't going our way, stop worrying about everything else and just worry about the game."—Coach Steve Kerr after the Warriors' 125-115 victory over the Pelicans, December 5, 2017*

During a regular season game against the New Orleans Pelicans, the Warriors were down by 20 points at halftime and could not seem to get into a rhythm on offense. Throughout the game, technical fouls were called against the Warriors as they got involved in heated arguments with the referees and some of the Pelicans players. Kevin Durant was ejected late in the game and Stephen Curry sprained his ankle. While they would eventually erase the 20-point deficit and win the game, what concerned Coach Kerr was not that they had to fight back to win this game, but rather how they played. They were emotionally reckless. He felt that the team lacked self-control, which led them to direct their emotions toward everyone and everything else besides their play on the court.

The goal of our opponent is to get us to lower our standards by engaging with them at their level. When we keep our composure and focus on our goals, we will be victorious. In order to maintain our poise while engaging with our rivals, we must be mindful of three actions that can lead to our demise. If we walk with the enemy and begin to apply their suggestions or advice, regardless of their success, that will be the start of us walking out of our purpose. Once we are not walking in purpose, we will eventually be out of alignment and standing in the direction of our opponent. This change in direction could ultimately lead to us no longer walking or standing, but rather sitting in their midst, away from our original destination. Whenever we walk, then stand, and then sit with our adversaries, we have lowered our standards and position—no longer standing upright but sitting.

A solution to keep our composure during challenges is to shift our focus back to the love of the game. The love of the game could be your motivation for starting your business or project, rekindling the spark of love that was the foundation of your marriage or relationship, or going back to what you first loved that drove your passion. Shifting your focus away from an individual and refocusing your attention on your "why" will anchor you and provide you with the calm to navigate through the storm. Remembering our first love will help us regain our composure to yield victory in due season. Winning is sacred.

**Action Point:** Be mindful of the company that you keep. Surround yourself with a tribe that feeds your vision and passion. Reject those who lead you away from fulfilling your purpose and promises over your lifespan.

**Declaration:** I have composure for the course and poise for the path in all areas of my life that yield a profit in the face of opposition.

# DAY 13:
# SHAPE

*"The defense, and the identity of our defense, and the rules of our defense is the biggest growth," Brown said. Those plays are commonplace for a team like the Warriors, but the Sixers have smaller guards and Embiid in the middle."—Rich Hofmann, The Athletic, on the Sixers' 89-80 victory over the Celtics, January 19, 2018*

Brett Brown, the former coach of the Philadelphia 76ers, praised the effort of his team's defense as one of the keys to victory in a game over the Boston Celtics. What made the Sixers' defense unique was that, like the Warriors, they employed switching strategy, but with smaller players and their seven-foot, All-Star center, Joel Embiid, who harassed players on the perimeter and in the post. The Warriors' defensive switching scheme utilized wing players, who were more versatile and able to guard multiple players, regardless of position. The Warriors employed this swarming defensive style, and it was instrumental in shaping their identity, as well as laying the foundation for securing multiple NBA titles. Other teams like the Sixers emulated this defensive technique but shaped it to fit their personnel.

When we see something that is working for someone else, there is nothing wrong with applying the principle to our own lives. However, the principle must reflect how we are divinely shaped. Pastor, author, and entrepreneur Keith Battle shares that we are shaped by our:

- **Spiritual Gifts/Superpowers**: These are what I am uniquely good at and that have been placed within me, whether it is serving others, speaking, teaching, providing strategy to organizations, etc.

- **Heart**: This is what I am passionate about and where I want to bring about change for the well-being of others.

- **Ability**: My strengths. What I am good at doing.

- **Personality**: A combination of characteristics that display my temperaments and how I respond to people and situations.

- **Experiences**: The things that I have survived, the joy that I have encountered, and the pain that I have overcome (Battle 2011).

*When we accept how we are shaped, we can then implement strategies that perfectly fit us, allowing us to be successful without compromise. In the same way every team cannot utilize switching concepts on the basketball court, we cannot all use identical principles the same ways in our own lives. We must tailor how we apply the ideas to fit our purpose based on how we are structured physically, mentally, and emotionally. Having the wisdom to honor who we are and humbly accept how we are created goes a long way toward making strides in the positive direction.*

**Action Point:** Embrace who you are and how you were uniquely created to fulfill your purpose. Find ways to bring your passion to life, by developing a plan that will help you use your abilities to bring joy to your life and others.

**Declaration:** I am fearfully and wonderfully made to reach my destiny.

# DAY 14: CULTURE

*"The two most important stretches of the game for the Warriors came at the start of the second and fourth quarters, with Curry in the locker room and Durant on the bench. The second-unit—with two-way player Quinn Cook serving as the point guard because of Shaun Livingston's DNP-rest night—opened the second on a 10-0 run, and the fourth on an 11-3 run. 'They've been great all season, getting leads back for us or pushing, stretching the leads,' Durant said. 'Defense and ball movement.'"—Anthony Slater, The Athletic, on the Warriors' 114-109 win over the Hawks, March 3, 2018*

Circumstances reveal our core values and the depths of our character. The foundation of our personal code of conduct and the healthy cultures that we develop within our lives, marriages, families, businesses, and endeavors is not established only when we win. In fact, we don't have a culture if we are only victorious in life. Winning does not define culture. Culture is defined by the day-to-day process of shaping and building our character. It becomes a part of the fabric of our daily lives that shines forth, even when everything is not going our way. In fact, we should rejoice when we face challenges and hardships because they provide the testing ground on which our personal tenets are tested—to see if they are solid as gold and able to be refined by fire.

The Warriors found themselves in a situation where two of their top players were not available at key points in the game. Instead of folding and conceding defeat, key members of their second unit were pivotal in leading them to victory. The Warriors experienced success because their team's play was anchored by two of their core values: defense and ball movement on offense. When the people were not available, the culture created within the organization sustained the team and allowed them to be triumphant. Adversity created the opportunity for the team to see that their core values could produce winning results.

No matter the challenges that we face in life, the result will be the development of core values that anchor us and lead us to achieve more than we can ever think or imagine, according to the power that works within us. Stay encouraged. Winning is sacred.

**Action Point**: Identify two core values in your life that you will nourish and cultivate daily.

**Declaration**: I give thanks in all circumstances because I am anchored and will not be moved.

# DAY 15: DEFENSE

*"I made my way to the middle and hit Draymond; he was streaking towards the lane. He drew the defense and kicked it back out to Klay in the corner. Bang. They called a timeout. I think we were up by 19. That was defense, pace, ball movement and unselfishness. That was Warriors basketball. It felt like we were back."—Shaun Livingston, "We Played for Each Other; That's Where the Passion Comes from," The Athletic, April 19, 2018*

The savvy veteran point guard Shaun Livingston identifies four core values that shaped the culture of the Warriors. He includes, in addition to defense and ball movement, pace and unselfishness. The four core values unveil the winning formula that made the Warriors unbeatable against formidable opponents. Livingston recalls a play against the San

Antonio Spurs in a first-round playoff series, where the Warriors were not quite themselves due to losing multiple games going into the playoffs. However, the catalyst that sparked a change for him was a defensive play by the center, Kevon Looney, that led to a fast break and an open three-point shot from marksman Klay Thompson.

Achieving enduring success in life is not fashioned by the style points we accumulate or our dazzling offensive prowess in our field of expertise. Rather it is honed by our activity on defense and what we defend. Defense initiates our offense. It protects what we hold dear. When we take the time to maintain and build up our faith, family, fitness, finances, and friendships, and make time for fun, we begin to live our whole lives. When we fail to defend these facets of our life, things can become chaotic, and we can become distracted, no longer focusing on the vision set before us. When we no longer move in faith to execute our mission that will bring our vision to fruition, that is when we can become defensive. And if we are defensive, there is a chance that we will offend others.

We were not created to be constantly on defense but rather to have systems in place so that we can be fruitful and enjoy the fruits of our labor. Being constantly on the defensive causes undue stress and does not allow us to appreciate the journey. How can we defend ourselves while simultaneously executing a strategic plan? The greatest defense that supports all areas of our lives is cultivating and maintaining our faith. Faith in something bigger than ourselves gives us the assurance that we can play offense without having to look over our backs. Taking care of our spiritual, mental, and emotional well-being through prayer and meditation gives us the ample tools we need to focus our attention on walking in our destiny. Protect your home court. Winning is sacred.

**Action Point:** Create a system that allows you to set goals for your faith, family, fitness, finances, field (career), friends, and fun.

**Declaration:** I am protected on every side. I walk by faith and not by sight.

# DAY 16:
# PACE

*"That was defense, pace, ball movement and unselfishness. That was Warriors basketball. It felt like we were back."*
—*Shaun Livingston, The Athletic, April 19, 2018*

The fact that Shaun Livingston even played a major role on the Warriors' championship teams is a testament to his character. Three years after being drafted out of high school by the Los Angeles Clippers in the 2004 NBA draft, Livingston experienced one of the most devastating injuries in sports when he tore his ACL, PCL, MCL, lateral meniscus, and dislocated his tibiofemoral joint and his kneecap. Medical doctors considered amputating his leg. His basketball career was in jeopardy, let alone his overall health. His road to recovery was daunting, as he had to relearn how to walk and regain basketball movement if he was ever going to play again.

Livingston returned to the basketball court 20 months after his injury and played his first game as a member of the Miami Heat. And while his playing time was limited, he did not wallow in self-pity, but rather his time on the court reassured him that he once again could play at a high level. This renewed sense of confidence sustained him throughout his basketball journey, leading him to the Warriors as a backup point guard. All the trials and tribulations that Livingston endured produced a resounding level of perseverance in his ability to overcome seemingly insurmountable odds. Perseverance strengthened and fortified his character, and character is the essential ingredient for a leader to facilitate and orchestrate a winning pace for their personal life, relationships, family, and team.

After a defensive stop, teammates look to find a leader who can bring the ball up the court with speed to set up the offense while attacking the weaknesses in an opponent's defensive design. What better person to bring the ball up the court with pace than someone with character, someone like Livingston? When we are a person of character, we infuse others with hope and hope is rooted in trust, which is why their teammates give them the ball. Character is not perfectionism, but rather the ability to be grateful in every situation and make the decision to move forward, despite shortcomings, flaws, and uncertainty. Leaders with character recognize a suitable pace that utilizes everyone's own unique gift for the benefit of the team, relationship, or family unit. Character recognizes that it is not about me. It doesn't go too fast or too slow, but rather is intentional about moving at the exact speed that will achieve success. Developing character is the secret to sustained success. Pace yourself. Winning is sacred.

**Action Point:** Take the time to consistently develop your character by learning from your mistakes and hardships, as well as what you have done right and your victories. They both are equally important.

**Declaration:** I have the pace to run the race with grace.

# DAY 17:
# MOVEMENT

*"He's been fantastic defensively. All over the place," Steve Kerr said. "This is a team that you have to disrupt. They're excellent with their execution until you have to try to take them out of things and Draymond is as good as anybody, I've ever seen in terms of recognizing a play and blowing it up."—Steve Kerr, Warriors' game three win over the San Antonio Spurs, April 19, 2018*

The Warriors' offense is predicated on ball movement and finding the best shot for an open player, preferably to one of their skilled perimeter shooters. On defense, the Warriors are also adept at stopping opponents from getting into an offensive flow. The ringleader of the Warriors' defense is Draymond Green, and what makes him special is that he is a master at causing disruption. Every NBA offense's goal is to set up and run their offense with precision, without any interference, to score as many points as possible to win the game. The defense's main objective is to create barriers for the offense to score and to get the ball back. The Warriors' ability to space the court with lethal 3-point shooters, who feed off accurate ball movement, makes it difficult for defenses to disrupt their motion. The Spurs, like other NBA teams, had an offensive scheme based on ball movement, but as former world champion boxer Mike Tyson once stated, "Everyone has a plan, until they get punched in the mouth." Draymond the Disruptor is that punch in the mouth and he stifles ball movement.

In our daily lives, the ball moves like this: We have a thought that leads to an action; an action becomes a habit; a habit leads to a lifestyle; and a lifestyle produces a destiny, a legacy. Everything starts with a thought, and our thoughts can produce an action that will lead either to victory or defeat. Whereas the goal on offense is to move the ball to score, the goal of a healthy thought life is to make sound decisions that lead to success—creating a legacy built on character. The issue is that sometimes our minds can seem like a combat zone, requiring our attention to make critical decisions in the face of daily disruptors such as worry, anxiety, fear, anger, doubt, past hurts, etc. These disruptors stop the flow of the ball in our life, causing havoc in our thought processes and making it hard to execute an action plan.

Therefore, it is critical that we sow ideas and concepts that speak life and enduring wisdom into our thoughts. Knowledge that has stood the test of time can equip our thoughts with a solid foundation, producing winning results that can give us an edge on the battlefield of the mind. In life, we will face obstacles that may upset the flow of our daily lives. But when we build our thought life up with convictions that are noble and pure, leading to a legacy, we will be victorious.

**Action Point:** Identify the one thing that you want to leave as your final legacy and feed your thought life with the prerequisite materials to reach that destination.

**Declaration:** My thoughts shall reap what I sow.

# DAY 18: UNSELFISHNESS

"*Though the Warriors emerged from the first quarter with a four-point lead, they'd yet to face a long stretch, against 'back-ups' Montrezl Harrell and Lou Williams. In not getting separation against weaker lineups, the Warriors left themselves vulnerable to what followed.*"—Ethan Strauss, "*The Warriors Identity: Back-to-Back Champs between Letdowns,*" *The Athletic, May 25, 2019*

To reach higher heights and achieve greatness in any area of life, we must be willing to make the hard decision to separate from the habits, activities, and thoughts that do not align with where we are going. This new behavior may cause some to call you selfish when they see a difference in your behavior that limits their influence or proximity to your life. If we do not recognize the importance of creating distance from negative practices and people to experience a new realm of distinction, we may wallow in mediocrity and not be our best selves, limiting our potential to return to help those we initially separated from in the beginning. This unfortunate state is the epitome of being selfish anytime we refuse to disconnect from anyone or anything that is hindering our personal growth.

Separation is necessary, as it is the prerequisite before achieving a breakthrough. Before one can experience advancement, there must be a time of deep concentration, pruning, and dedication to oneself to detach from anyone or anything that may be hindering forward progress. The Warriors were not in a flow against the Los Angeles Clippers during a playoff game, and while they were in the lead, they did not create enough distance between themselves and the Clippers on the scoreboard and only had a four-point lead after the first quarter. The Warriors had the talent to win the game, but by not creating enough separation against a weaker opponent, the Warriors allowed the Clippers to be competitive and eventually win the game.

There are many factors that may contribute to us not achieving our goals or reaching the desired outcome. Some factors are beyond our control.

However, what we can control is our desire to go higher to reach greater heights in our personal lives, relationships, and endeavors. This requires a deeper commitment and call to relinquish everything that we hold dear, making ourselves self-less. When we embrace and grow to love who we are, that is the ultimate breakthrough. Winning is sacred.

**Action Point:** Schedule time to take a personal retreat to a secluded place (it can be as simple as a room within your home or away somewhere else) and identify thoughts, mindsets, and behaviors that you need to separate from in order to flourish and thrive.

**Declaration:** I break away to prepare and possess my breakthrough.

# DAY 19:
# START FAST

"*The Warriors lost the second quarter by two, won the third quarter by three and lost the fourth quarter by one. In those 36 combined minutes, the score was even. But they lost by 15 because they lost the first quarter by 15, which has been a common theme this season. After Thursday night, the Warriors are now a cumulative minus-142 in their 36 first quarters. Among all teams, it's the second-worst cumulative quarter performance in the league this season.*

*1. Hawks: minus-169 in first quarters*

*2. Warriors: minus-142 in first quarters*

*3. Cavaliers: minus-140 in second quarters*"
—*Anthony Slater, "Five Observations: Warriors Lose to Timberwolves, Sit Alone with NBA's Second-Worst Record," The Athletic, January 2, 2020*

Fools live by the year—they count the years and make plans based on yearly resolutions or goals. Wise people live by the day, adjusting their yearly plans to achieve success. However, those who excel live by the minute. They make sure that they do not waste time to make the most of each moment. Make every minute count this year.

The 2020–2021 Warriors struggled to score points and play solid defense in the first quarters of games, which quickly led them to be overmatched by their opponents, succumbing to a losing season. Not only must we use time as an ally to achieve victory, but it is also imperative that we grow our sphere of influence within our areas of expertise by being able to solve problems and maintaining a defensive stronghold to protect our emotional, physical, and spiritual well-being. When we can solve problems that hinder us from progressing, this is the equivalent of scoring points on offense. However, we cannot solely focus on offense. We must put the same effort and energy into defending what we have gained through consistent hard work, before it is lost. Being fruitful is not only about producing, but it also requires that our fruit and the process that we use to produce the fruit remain intact. If the fruit we produce escapes through our hands with nothing to show for our labor, that is a sign that we may need to modify our defensive strategy.

When our ability to score on offense while making key stops on defense flows in unison in our life, we can get a head start over the adversary, leading us to victory. Exceed your expectations by starting fast, being solution-oriented, and creating a stronghold to protect your lane. Winning is sacred.

**Action Point:** Develop a personal plan that allows you to prosper and protect the fruit of your labor.

**Declaration:** I am equipped to excel and go beyond my expectations.

# DAY 20:
# CHAOS

*"Kevin Durant walked out of Charlotte with the 2019 All-Star Game MVP, and it's not really a bad choice. Durant scored 31 points and was responsible for six threes. Thirty 'quiet' points in the middle of chaos. Nothing out of the ordinary and no different from a regular season game."*
*—Jannelle Moore, SBNation: Golden State of Mind, February 18, 2019*

The 68th edition of the NBA All-Star game in Charlotte, North Carolina, was filled, as usual, with the NBA's best and brightest stars. It featured Team LeBron, led by LeBron James, with Kevin Durant and Kyrie Irving, versus Team Giannis, captained by Giannis Antetokounmpo, featuring Stephen Curry and Joel Embiid. Like most all-star games, the teams did not employ a specific strategy to counteract the opposition. It was simply a friendly competition among the world's best players throughout most of the game, until the closing minutes of the final quarter when each team's coaches installed a game plan best suited to achieve victory for their squad.

Due to the lack of a consistent game plan, chaos ensued during the game due to a lack of structure. In warfare, the opposing side may employ chaos to cause distractions and disrupt the plan of the opposition. Chaos is the seed that is planted to create confusion with the desired outcome to kill, steal, and/or destroy. Therefore, it is paramount that whenever we sense uncertainty, we observe and identify the root cause of where chaos has been introduced in an area of life, whether it be our marriages, families, relationships, career, health, business, finances, ministry, etc. Once the source of chaos has been identified, that is the exact moment when we introduce a system to that area of our life to bring forth order and efficiency.

Durant was right in the center of the storm, surrounded by the world's best athletes during the All-Star game, but he never wavered. He stayed steadfast and centered, relying on what has carried him throughout his career, whether in the regular season or championship playoff runs. What allowed Durant to flourish during the chaos? Durant's quiet yet ever-efficient system of scoring at all three levels of the basketball court: in the post, the mid-range, and the three-point shot. Staying committed to his system allowed him to outshine his peers during the chaos.

We all may not have the athletic skill and scoring ability of Durant, but we do have something that is specifically tailored to us that makes us unique and gifted in our families, communities, and beyond. Being skilled and gifted will not carry us through a storm. When challenges arise, the victors have a system in place that quickly transfers order and structure to the battlefield. The system then creates an outlet for our talents and strengths to be released so that we can overcome any obstacles that were designed to throw us off track. A well-developed system diffuses chaos and guarantees victory. Winning is sacred.

**Action Point:** Identify one of your strengths and develop a system around that strength that you can employ whenever you face or sense turmoil.

**Declaration:** Order is pleasure.

# DAY 21: TRANSITION

*"One of the issues with the absence of Green is the Warriors don't push in transition. That's Green's specialty. But while bracing for impact in the paint, the Warriors have been crawling up the court."—Marcus Thompson, Warriors Once Again Show That, for them, size doesn't matter, The Athletic, February 11, 2022*

Warrior nation waited with anticipation, during the 2021–2022 season, for the return of Klay Thompson after his two-year absence returning from a torn left ACL during the NBA Finals in 2019 and a torn Achilles tendon from the offseason of 2020. The sharpshooter was sorely missed this time, and his return to the court on January 9, 2022, brought back hope of championship aspirations for the franchise. While Klay's return was a cause for celebration, one of his running mates, Draymond Green, was sidelined due to a back injury tied to his hamstring. Over the course of a few games, the Warriors felt the impact of Green's leave as the team struggled to play with speed and could not get into their transition game, which made it hard for their offense to score points easily.

Transition is the process or a period of changing from one state or condition to another. It requires movement. When we experience a transition in our lives, it can sometimes create a level of uncertainty as we move from what is familiar to the unfamiliar. Transition gives birth to opportunity, but if fear paralyzes us due to attachment to what makes us feel comfortable and we don't move with urgency, we could miss out on the opportunity. Transition is necessary, because it puts us in a position to move to the next level to fulfill our purpose and reach our destiny.

This is what makes Green special. He seizes the opportunity and is not afraid to take advantage of chances that put his team in a position to be successful. A second-round draft pick and considered undersized for his position, he uses what is perceived as a weakness to ignite transition. Bigger players in his position cannot keep up with him, which makes their team a liability when the Warriors are playing at full speed. What makes us unique are the tools that carry us through seasons of transition and give us a distinct advantage when we are moving to the next level.

Regardless of his size, Green's desire to play with speed to drive transition is his heart. The cradle of transition and movement in the face of change is the heart. A heart that is constantly fueled by faith, despite barriers and circumstances, will quench fear and initiate transition. The heart is the seat of our emotions and must be kept and nurtured at all costs. The heart exposes our motives and out of it flows the issues of our life. However, when the heart is imprinted with faith, nothing shall be impossible. Knowing that all things are possible gives us the strength to move in the face of uncertainty. A pure heart will see and experience victory.

**Action Point:** Prepare your heart for transition. It's time to move.

**Declaration:** I was created for more. I am no longer a servant, but an heir to the promise set for my life and the lives of my loved ones. Winning is sacred.

# CONCLUSION

Thank you for taking this 21-day journey along with me, identifying the keys to the success of the NBA World Champions, the Golden State Warriors. Please feel free to go back to revisit any idea that resonated with you and meditate on it daily to stay connected with yourself, your loved ones, and your community. These qualities are timeless, and wisdom has no end date. Seasons change, but the appropriate application of wisdom transcends time. I celebrate your growth, victory, perpetual peace, and willingness to invest in your success. Winning is sacred.

# BIBLIOGRAPHY

1. Battle, Keith. "What's in Your Bag?" *Zion Church Landover*, 25 Sept. 2011, https://zionlandover.com/sermon/575-whats-in-your-bag.

2. Friedell, Nick. "Kevin Durant, DeMarcus Cousins Ejected After Brief Dust-Up." ESPN. ESPN Internet Ventures, December 5, 2017. https://www.espn.com/nba/story/_/id/21672227/kevin-durant-golden-state-warriors-ejected-again-got-more-poised.

3. Hofmann, Rich. "The Rewind: Embiid's Brilliance, Switching Defense Allow Sixers to Salvage Ugly Game in Boston." The Athletic, January 19, 2018. https://theathletic.com/216175/2018/01/19/the-rewind-embiids-brilliance-switching-defense-allow-sixers-to-salvage-ugly-game-in-boston/.

4. Letourneau, Connor. "Without Kevin Durant, Warriors Showcase Depth in Rout of Minnesota." SFGATE. San Francisco Chronicle, November 9, 2017. https://www.sfgate.com/warriors/article/Warriors-showcase-depth-in-rout-of-Minnesota-12343492.php.

5. Livingston, Shaun. "Shaun Livingston: 'We Played for Each Other; That's Where the Passion Comes From'." The Athletic. The Athletic, April 19, 2018. https://theathletic.com/320749/2018/04/19/shaun-

livingston-we-played-for-each-other-thats-where-the-passion-comes-from/.

6. Medina, Mark. "Warriors Overcome Sluggish Start to Down New Orleans 128-120." East Bay Times. East Bay Times, October 21, 2017. https://www.eastbaytimes.com/2017/10/20/warriors-overcome-sluggish-start-to-down-new-orleans-128-120/.

7. Medina, Mark. "What Went Wrong in Warriors' 122-121 Loss to Rockets." *The Mercury News*. The Mercury News, October 18, 2017. https://www.mercurynews.com/2017/10/18/what-went-wrong-in-warriors-122-121-loss-to-rockets/.

8. Moore, Jannelle. "Team Giannis Collapses in All Star Game, Overblown Reactions Ensue." Golden State Of Mind. SBNATION, February 18, 2019. https://www.goldenstateofmind.com/2019/2/18/18228987/nba-all-star-game-2019-kevin-durant-steph-curry-team-giannis-vs-team-lebron.

9. Nadkarni, Andrew Sharp and Rohan. "One Telling Stat for All 30 NBA Teams." Sports Illustrated. Sports Illustrated, October 20, 2017. https://www.si.com/nba/2017/10/20/nba-preview-statistics-numbers-warriors-cavs-celtics-rockets.

10. Slater, Anthony. "Five Observations from the Warriors' 114-109 Win Over the Hawks." The Athletic. The Athletic, March 3, 2018. https://theathletic.com/259914/2018/03/03/five-observations-from-the-warriors-114-109-win-over-the-hawks/.

11. Slater, Anthony. "Five Observations from the Warriors' 110-97 Game 3 Win Over the Spurs." The Athletic,

April 20, 2018. https://theathletic.com/321878/2018/04/20/five-observations-from-the-warriors-110-97-game-3-win-over-the-spurs/.

12. Slater, Anthony. "Five Observations from the Warriors' 110-106 Loss to the Kings." The Athletic, November 27, 2017. https://theathletic.com/167851/2017/11/28/five-observations-from-the-warriors-110-106-loss-to-the-kings/.

13. Slater, Anthony. "Five Observations: Warriors Lose to Timberwolves, Sit Alone with NBA's Second-Worst Record." The Athletic, January 2, 2020. https://theathletic.com/1505225/2020/01/02/five-observations-warriors-lose-to-timberwolves-sit-alone-with-nbas-second-worst-record/.

14. Strauss, Ethan Sherwood. "Bring the Noise: Stephen Curry Puts Warriors Back on Track." ESPN. ESPN Enterprises, March 5, 2017. https://www.espn.in/blog/golden-state-warriors/post/_/id/3923/bring-the-noise-stephen-curry-puts-warriors-back-on-track.

15. Strauss, Ethan. "The Warriors Identity: Back-to-Back Champs, between Letdowns." The Athletic. The Athletic, April 25, 2019. https://theathletic.com/945114/2019/04/25/the-warriors-identity-back-to-back-champs-between-letdowns/.

16. Strauss, Ethan Sherwood. "With a Needed Boost from Andre Iguodala, Warriors Win 12th in Row." ESPN. ESPN Internet Ventures, November 29, 2016. https://www.espn.com/blog/golden-state-warriors/post/_/id/2908/with-a-needed-boost-from-andre-iguodala-warriors-win-12th-in-row.

17. Thompson, Marcus. "Thompson: The Stephen Curry 20-Point Quarter in Philadelphia - Remember Those? Here's Why They've Been Rare Recently." The Athletic. The Athletic, November 19, 2017. https://theathletic. com/159911/2017/11/19/thompson-the-stephen-curry-20-point-quarter-remember-those-they-are-increasingly-rare/.

18. Thompson, Marcus. "Thompson: Warriors Once Again Show That, for Them, Size Still Doesn't Matter." The Athletic. The Athletic, February 11, 2022. https://theathletic. com/3124740/2022/02/11/thompson-warriors-once-again-show-that-for-them-size-still-doesnt-matter/.

19. Thompson, Marcus. "We Know, It's Early — But Still... the Warriors Aren't Quite That Team We're Used To." The Athletic, November 30, 2017. https://theathletic. com/170337/2017/11/30/thompson-we-know-its-early-but-still-the-warriors-arent-quite-that-team-were-used-to/.

# ABOUT THE AUTHOR

Jonas N. Strickland has been inspired by sports and sports journalism since he was a child growing up in Washington, D.C. and Boston. With more than fifteen years' experience in education, Strickland is a certified school librarian, mentor for young adults, and co-host of iHeartRadio's The HBCU Creative Podcast.

Strickland earned his bachelor of science at Lincoln University, his master of divinity at Howard University School of Divinity, and his master of library and information science at Kent State University. In 2022, he was named the Mikva Challenge D.C. Educator of the Year and the Build D.C. Educator of the Year.

Strickland lives with his wife, April, and their three children, Capri, Lawrence, and Harper, in Washington, D.C. In his spare time, he enjoys reading fantasy novels, listening to podcasts, and watching sports and anime. He is passionate about uplifting historically Black colleges and universities.

To connect, email him at:
jonasnkosi@gmail.com

## CREATING DISTINCTIVE BOOKS
## WITH INTENTIONAL RESULTS

We're a collaborative group of creative masterminds
with a mission to produce high-quality books to position
you for monumental success in the marketplace.

Our professional team of writers, editors, designers,
and marketing strategists work closely together to ensure
that every detail of your book is a clear representation
of the message in your writing.

### Want to know more?
Write to us at info@publishyourgift.com
or call (888) 949-6228

Discover great books, exclusive offers, and more at
**www.PublishYourGift.com**

Connect with us on social media

@publishyourgift